MW01194807

Presented To

_____

From

_____

Date

_____

ZONDERKIDZ

I Wonder: Exploring God's Grand Story
Copyright © 2021 by Glenys Nellist
Illustrations © 2021 by Alessandra Fusi

Requests for information should be addressed to:

Zonderkidz, 3900 Sparks Drive SE, Grand Rapids, Michigan 49546

Hardcover ISBN 978-0-310-76830-2
Ebook ISBN 978-0-310-76838-8

All Scripture quotations, unless otherwise indicated are taken from the Holy Bible, *New International Reader's Version*®, NIrV®. Copyright © 1995, 1996, 1998, 2014 by Biblica, Inc.® Used by permission of Zondervan. All rights reserved worldwide. www.zondervan.com. The "NIrV" and "New International Reader's Version" are trademarks registered in the United States Patent and Trademark Office by Biblica, Inc.®

Any internet addresses (websites, blogs, etc.) and telephone numbers in this book are offered as a resource. They are not intended in any way to be or imply an endorsement by Zondervan, nor does Zondervan vouch for the content of these sites and numbers for the life of this book.

No part of this publication may be reproduced, stored in a retrieval system, or transmitted in any form or by any means—electronic, mechanical, photocopy, recording, or any other—except for brief quotations in printed reviews, without the prior permission of the publisher.

Zonderkidz is a trademark of Zondervan.

Art direction and design: Kris Nelson/StoryLook Design

Printed in Korea

21 22 23 24 25 26 27 /SAM/ 15 14 13 12 11 10 9 8 7 6 5 4 3 2 1

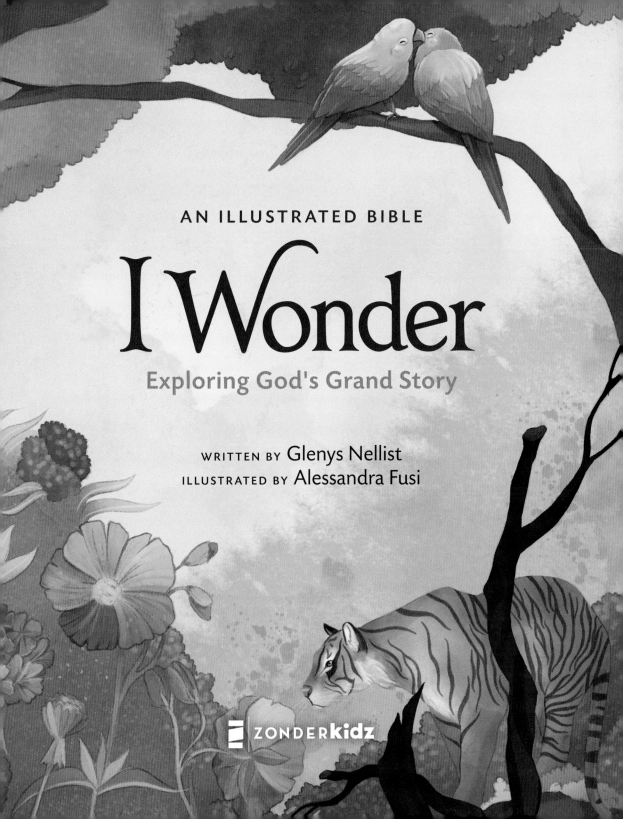

AN ILLUSTRATED BIBLE

I Wonder

Exploring God's Grand Story

WRITTEN BY **Glenys Nellist**

ILLUSTRATED BY **Alessandra Fusi**

ZONDER**kidz**

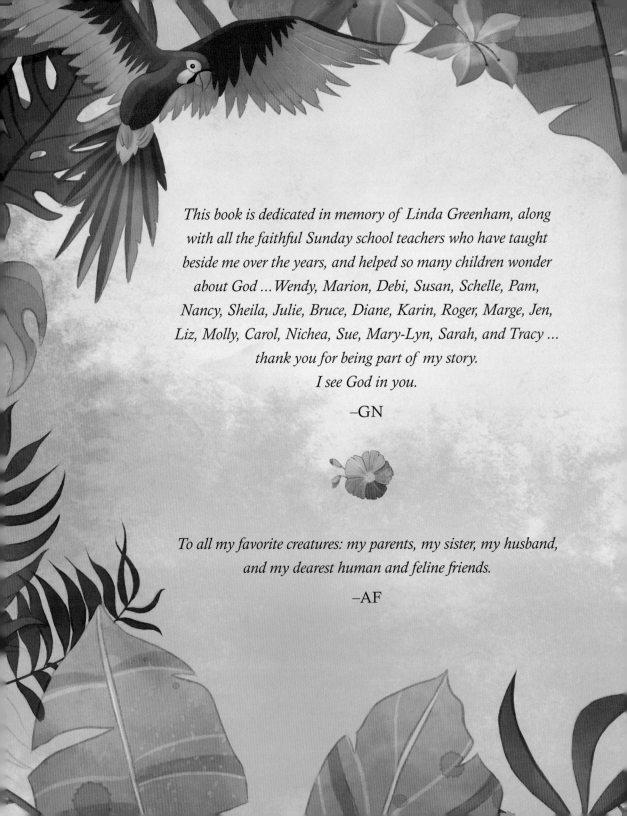

This book is dedicated in memory of Linda Greenham, along with all the faithful Sunday school teachers who have taught beside me over the years, and helped so many children wonder about God …Wendy, Marion, Debi, Susan, Schelle, Pam, Nancy, Sheila, Julie, Bruce, Diane, Karin, Roger, Marge, Jen, Liz, Molly, Carol, Nichea, Sue, Mary-Lyn, Sarah, and Tracy … thank you for being part of my story.
I see God in you.

–GN

To all my favorite creatures: my parents, my sister, my husband, and my dearest human and feline friends.

–AF

A Note from the Author

The Bible truly is a "wonder-full" book. From the first page to the last, the Bible is filled with stories of ordinary people who encountered an extraordinary God. Some stories are hard to understand; some make us scratch our heads; some make us laugh or cry; but *all* of them make us wonder. As you read about God's activity and presence in the lives of these ordinary people, I invite you to pause and ask such questions as:

I wonder who God is …

I wonder where God is …

I wonder what God looks like …

I wonder what God's voice sounds like …

I wonder what God wants me to do in the world …

As you ponder these deep questions, the most important one to ask is: *I wonder how I am part of God's great story* … because you are.

Glenys Nellist ♡

—Glenys Nellist

OLD TESTAMENT

New Testament

OLD TESTAMENT

I wonder about
CREATION

Genesis 1:1–27 and 2:7

No one heard the Word. The birds didn't hear it. The trees didn't hear it. The mountains didn't hear it ... because they had not been created yet. The Word came soft, like a whisper when there was nothing. The Word came into an empty world where it hovered and hung over the darkness of the deep. And just for a moment, there was nothing but silence. And when the time was just right, God's voice echoed into the silence and whispered the world into being.

"Let there be light."

And an amazing thing happened.

The light was listening. The light heard the Word.
And the light came. The light came—flooding and
leaping and dancing into the darkness, chasing away all the
shadows and shining into every corner. And it was *so* good!

After that, there was no stopping God! At the sound of God's voice, the sky spread her wide wings and flew into place. The oceans roared as they rushed and ran and filled the valleys with churning foam. The mountains groaned and jostled and heaved as they pushed their tips upward and pierced the clouds. And down below, grass became green and trees grew tall and strong.

Fish splashed in the oceans and eagles soared through blue skies. Monkeys swung from tree to tree as caterpillars crept and sloths slept. There were wriggles and roars and stomps and snores; screeches and howls and gallops and growls. And God's wonderful world was filled from top to bottom with wonderful life. Everywhere God looked, every bit of space and every corner of creation was filled with the sounds and colors and movements of life. And it was all so very good.

God smiled. The world was ready now—ready for what God was about to do next. And the whole world held its breath and watched in wonder as God bent down, scooped up the dust of the earth, and blew on it gently with the breath of life.

And from the dust, in the palm of God's own hand, God's children were born.

I Wonder

... if God still whispers.

... which part of creation God enjoyed the most.

... how God could make life out of dust.

... how far God had to bend down to reach the dust.

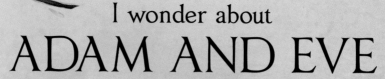

I wonder about
ADAM AND EVE

Genesis 3:1–24

Adam and Eve stepped down from the palm of God's hand. Where were they? God's brand-new children held their breath and gazed in wonder. Was this gorgeous garden their home? Under a cloudless azure sky, birds perched high in the treetops and sang their morning song, as though they were welcoming Adam and Eve into the world. It seemed as if the flowers danced at their feet and the trees bowed their branches down in greeting. The river nearby bubbled and sparkled as it ran, and all the leaves shimmered and waved their hello in the breeze.

Everywhere God's children looked they saw a rainbow of colors as sunlight peeped through the leaves and shone on the butterflies as they fluttered in the wind.

"Is this our home?" Eve gasped.

"Yes," God whispered. "It's yours, Eve. I made it for you and Adam."

Eve laughed and grabbed Adam's hand as they ran, barefoot, across the lush, green grass that spread out, like a carpet, under their feet.

God smiled and watched in delight as Adam and Eve began to explore their new home. But God wasn't the only one who was watching. From his hiding place in a hole in the ground, a jealous, sneaky snake spied on God's children. And when he was ready, he made his move …

Sneaking quietly through the grass, the snake made his way toward the tree where Eve stood. She was looking up into its branches and admiring its fruit.

"Don't you want to taste that delicious fruit?" the snake hissed.

"Oh, I do!" Eve said. "But I can't. This is the one fruit God told us not to eat. If we eat it, we'll die."

"Oh, I don't think that's really true," the snake replied. "The only reason God doesn't want you to eat that fruit is because this is the Tree of Knowledge. If you eat from it, you'll know everything. You'll be just like God."

Eve thought about that for a minute. God was wonderful. God was good. Surely if she could be like God that wouldn't be a bad thing? Eve plucked a piece of fruit. She tasted it. And then she gave some to Adam, while the snake snickered and slithered back into his hole. For the first time since Adam and Eve stepped into the lovely garden, the birds stopped singing. The flowers stopped dancing. Dark clouds crept in and covered the sun. And Adam and Eve were cold.

"What have we done?" they whispered. "We made the wrong choice. We shouldn't have done that." And they hid behind a bush.

Later that evening God walked into the garden, but Adam and Eve were nowhere to be found.

"Children," God called, "where are you?" Adam and Eve stepped out from their hiding place, but they couldn't look at God, because they knew they'd done wrong. God's heart filled with sadness. "Children! Why did you eat the fruit of the one tree I told you not to?" God's voice trembled as Adam and Eve began to cry. "You'll have to leave the garden now," God said, sadly. "But before you leave, I'm going to make clothes for you."

As Adam and Eve left the wonderful garden that had been their home, God covered them with more than just clothes. Even though they didn't know it, they were all wrapped up in God's love and grace and forgiveness and hope. Adam and Eve had done wrong. But God would find a way to make it right.

God closed the gate behind Adam and Eve. But as they stepped out into the world, they didn't go alone. God went with them. They were God's children. They would always be God's children. And wherever they went, God would go too.

I Wonder

... if God goes with me wherever I go.

... why God told Adam and Eve not to eat that fruit.

... if I'm covered in God's love and grace too.

I wonder about
NOAH

Genesis 6:1–22

Hundreds of years passed. Since the time Adam and Eve had left the garden and ventured out into the world, their family had grown and grown. Their children had children, grandchildren, and many great-grandchildren. But people were *still* making the wrong choices. Every day, God's heart grew more and more sad as the people on earth hurt each other. They chose hatred instead of love, and meanness instead of kindness. But God was watching someone special. His name was Noah. Noah was good and kind, and most of all, Noah loved God.

One day, God decided that the only way to fix the earth was to start all over again. And Noah was just the man to help.

"Noah," God said. "Listen carefully. I want you to build an ark, a huge boat, one that's big and strong enough to carry you, your family, and two of each kind of animal. It's going to rain for forty days. A flood will cover the whole earth and make it clean. And when the rain stops, and the water goes down, there will be a new home for you, your family, and all the animals."

Noah didn't know what to think. But he trusted God, and so he set to work, first gathering all the wood he could find. Day after day was spent cutting, carrying, hammering, sawing, sanding, and nailing—until finally, the huge boat was finished.

24

Noah gathered two of every kind of animal. They ran and scampered and waddled and soared and galloped until they were all safely settled inside the ark.

Noah and his family watched as huge, dark clouds swallowed up the sky and the rain began to fall.

But after forty days and forty nights afloat, the pitter-patter of rain stopped, the waters went down, and the ark came to rest on dry land.

Noah opened the door and all the animals rushed out, ready to find a new home. Noah stepped down from the boat and looked up into the sky. The clouds had gone. And in their place was a shining rainbow that stretched over the whole earth, as far and as high and as wide as Noah could see.

"You don't need to worry, Noah," God said. "There'll never be another flood like that again. This is our new start. Today is a new day. This is a new earth. And we have new hope."

As Noah fell asleep that night under a cloudless, starlit sky, he knew that God was with him—God, who was making all things new.

I Wonder

... if God still makes new things.

... if God loves seeing rainbows as much as I do.

... how Noah's wife felt about it all.

I wonder about
ABRAHAM AND SARAH

Genesis 12:2–7; 15:1–7; 17:1–16

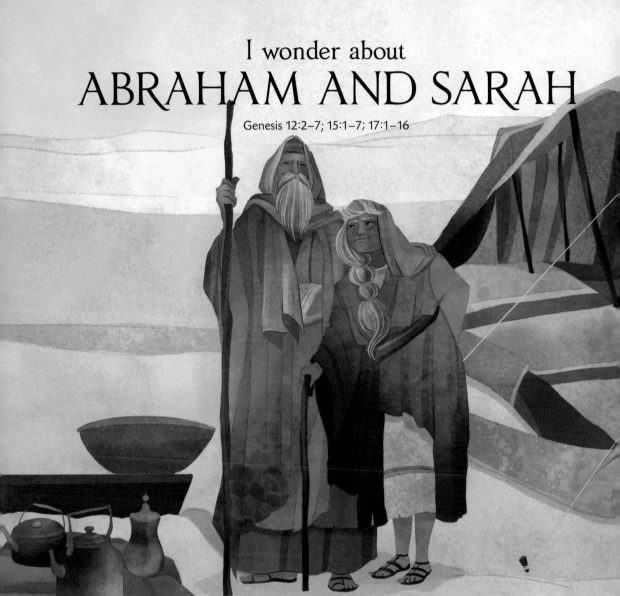

Long after Noah and his family left the ark, God met a new friend named Abram. Abram was a very old man. His hair was gray. His beard was long. His wife, Sarai, was a very old lady. Her hair was gray. Her back was bent.

More than anything else in the whole world, Abram and Sarai wanted a son. But they were far too old. It was impossible. But one special night, God had a big surprise for Abram.

"Abram," God whispered. "Come outside with me. Look up at the stars. Can you count them?"

Abram gazed up at the stars twinkling above. He pointed his finger and started to count. "One, two, three, four, five, six, seven, eight, nine, ten ..." Abram couldn't keep up! It seemed like the more he gazed into the darkness, the more stars peeped out from their hiding places.

> Five stars here, six stars there,
> Seven stars, eight stars, stars everywhere!
> Stars that were big, stars that were small,
> Stars, stars everywhere—he couldn't count them all!

"God," Abram said. "This is making me dizzy. There must be more than a million stars in the sky. How can I possibly count them all?"

"You can't," God chuckled. "And guess what? You won't be able to count all the people in your great big family either. Just like these stars, there will be more than a million of them. You and Sarai will have a son called Isaac. He will have children and grandchildren and great-grandchildren.

"Your family will grow and grow and spread out across the whole earth. And I will bless them. They will live here, Abram. All the land that you can see, from the north to the south, from the east to the west—all of it will be their home. This is my promise to you."

What? Abram was astonished! He was going to be a daddy! Sarai was going to be a mommy! And, as if that wasn't enough to get excited about, God had another surprise for Abram. "Your new name will be Abraham, and your wife's name will be Sarah. I will bless you and be with you, and your special family will be my special family too."

Abraham's heart filled with joy and thanksgiving as he fell to his knees in prayer. His life was not over yet! God had found a way where there had seemed to be no way. God had promised him a new name, a new baby, a new family, and a whole new future.

And God kept those promises. Because God always does …

I Wonder

... how many stars were twinkling that night.

... how Sarah felt when she found out she was going to be a mommy.

... if God still does impossible things.

I wonder about
JACOB

Genesis 28:10–22

Abraham's grandson was running as fast as he could. Jacob had to run fast, and he couldn't stop. If he did, his brother, Esau, might catch up with him and hurt him. Jacob had cheated his brother, and that was wrong, but Jacob didn't know how to make it right. And so, Jacob ran far into the night, away from his home, until he couldn't run anymore.

The sun was going down. It was cold and dark. Jacob was tired. He looked around to see if he could find somewhere warm and cozy to rest, but there was nothing there. This was the desert. There were no trees overhead to shelter him, no soft grass to lie on, no cave to crawl into. So Jacob lay down on the hard ground, put his head on a big, hard rock, and went to sleep.

But as he slept, Jacob had the most wonderful dream. There, in front of him, was a huge golden stairway that stretched all the way up through the clouds. Where could that staircase lead? Just as Jacob was thinking about climbing the stairs, he saw beautiful angels floating up and down them. And at the very top of the staircase, where the light shimmered and sparkled and shone as bright as the sun, God was standing. Jacob could not believe it—he was peeking through the gates of heaven!

"Jacob," God said, "listen to me. I'm the God of your family. I'm the God of your grandfather, Abraham, and the God of your father, Isaac. I'm your God too. I will bless you and be with you. I'll never leave you, and one day you'll be able to come back to your home. Your family will be many in number and will spread out across this whole land, as far as you can see, from the north to the south, from the east to the west."

Wow! Jacob recognized that promise! That was the same promise God had given to his Grandpa Abraham. God was here—even though Jacob hadn't known it.

When Jacob woke from his sleep, he jumped up. What could he do to say thank you to God? Jacob took the rock he'd slept on, stood it tall, and poured oil on it. Then he knelt in the sand and prayed, "Thank you, God, for always being with me, even when I don't know it."

Jacob felt so much better. He had rested. He had met God in this special place. And maybe one day, God would show him how to put things right with his brother. Jacob was ready for the next part of his journey. It was morning. It was a new day.

I Wonder

... what I might see if I could look through the gates of heaven.

... if God is with me even when I don't know it.

... why Jacob stood that stone up and poured oil on it when he prayed.

I wonder about
ESAU

Genesis 32–33

Many years passed. Jacob became rich. He got married. He had a good life. But he still thought about the brother he'd cheated. One morning, God said to him, "Today's the day, Jacob. It's time to go home. It's time to put things right with your brother. Go, and I will be with you." Jacob was very nervous. His brother might kill him! Jacob called his servant and said, "Take a message to my brother Esau. Tell him I own hundreds of camels, cows, sheep, goats, and donkeys, and I'm ready to share them all."

But when the servant came back, he had bad news. "Get ready, Jacob," he said. "Esau's on his way to meet you, and he's not alone. He has four hundred men with him."

Oh, no! Jacob trembled with fear. He fell to his knees and prayed. "Oh, God of my family, God of my grandfather Abraham, God of my father Isaac, you have been so good to me. You promised that my family would be vast. You promised that I'd be able to go home one day. Please, save me from my brother."

Jacob felt much better after he'd prayed. He remembered that God had promised never to leave him. Then Jacob thought of a clever plan. He would send his servants to meet Esau first. They could go before him with presents for his brother, then maybe Esau wouldn't hurt him. He called the first servant and said, "You will be in the lead. Go to my brother and take these two hundred and twenty goats. When he asks who they're for, tell him they are a special gift from me."

The second servant was next in line, with two hundred and twenty sheep; then the third servant followed with thirty camels and their babies. The fourth servant had fifty cows and the fifth servant had thirty donkeys. Five servants set out ahead of Jacob.

As the sun rose early the next morning, Jacob set out, trembling with fear. There, over the hill, was Esau, charging toward him with his four hundred men. Jacob was terrified! Esau lifted his arms high in the air and … gave Jacob a huge hug! It was the best hug Jacob had ever had! "Jacob!" his brother laughed. "I don't want goats. I don't want sheep. I don't want camels with their babies. I just want a hug from my brother!"

Jacob couldn't believe it! He cupped Esau's face in his hands and looked into his brother's eyes as they filled with tears. And as he looked into Esau's face, Jacob thought he saw the face of God. In that moment, Jacob knew that his clever plan hadn't saved him. His animals hadn't saved him. God had.

I Wonder

... if I can see God's face in others.

... if others see God's face when they look at me.

... if God still makes promises.

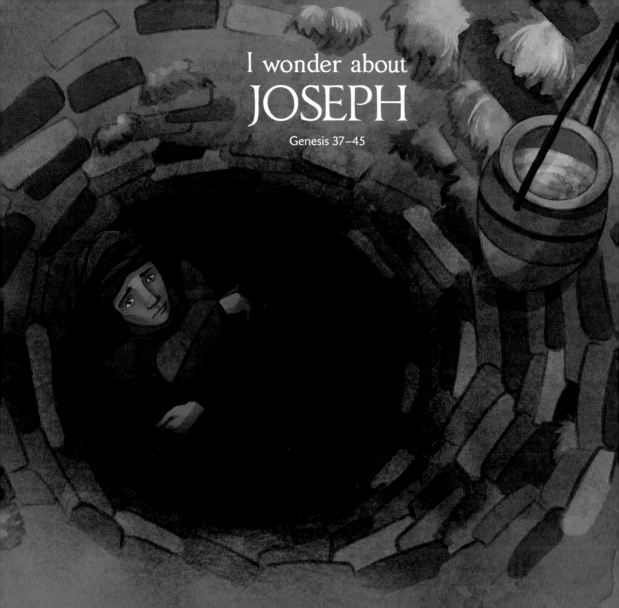

I wonder about
JOSEPH

Genesis 37–45

In the bottom of a deep, dark well, Joseph sat and hugged his knees. He was cold and wet, and he shivered in fright. Why had his brothers thrown him down here? Why had they stolen the beautiful new coat that Jacob, his father, had made for him? Why did his brothers hate him so much? But Joseph already knew the answer to *that* question. His brothers were jealous of him. He was their father's favorite, and he was the only one who could understand dreams and tell people what they meant.

Joseph thought back to the dream he'd had only a few nights before, when the sun and the moon and eleven stars had bowed down in front of him. Maybe he shouldn't have told his eleven brothers what it meant—that one day they would all bow down to him. But it was too late now. Joseph closed his eyes and prayed. It was all he could do. He knew that no matter how bad things were, God was with him.

When he heard voices above his head, Joseph scrambled to his feet. Perhaps they had just been teaching him a lesson, and now he could go home. But as they pulled him out of the pit, Joseph heard one of his brothers talking to some men. "Here. You can have him for twenty shekels of silver. Take him with you to Egypt."

Joseph closed his eyes and prayed as the traders dragged him away. It was all he could do.

In Egypt, Joseph worked for Potiphar, an important man in the king's army. Joseph worked so hard and was so good at everything he did that it wasn't long before Potiphar put him in charge of his whole household. At long last, things were going well for Joseph! But one day Potiphar's wife decided that she liked Joseph better than her husband.

"I'm sorry," Joseph said, as she followed him around the house. "You're married to Potiphar. I can't spend time with you."

But Potiphar's wife hated to be ignored! One day she came up with a wicked plan. She told lies about Joseph and had him thrown into jail.

Many years passed by until one night Pharaoh, the king of Egypt, had a very strange dream. He shouted for his advisors. "Bring me the wisest men and all the finest magicians in Egypt. I need to know the meaning of my dream."

But none of the wise men or the magicians could explain what Pharaoh's dream meant.

"King," said his cupbearer, "when I was in jail a long time ago, I met a wise man called Joseph. He knew the meaning of dreams. Perhaps he can help you."

So Joseph was brought to the king. "Is it true you can understand dreams?" Pharaoh asked.

"Only God can do that," said Joseph. "But if you tell me your dream, God will help us find the answer."

"I was standing by the river," said the king. "And I saw something awful. Seven ugly cows came out of the water and ate seven big cows."

"Oh, King," said Joseph. "It means that the next seven years in Egypt will be good ones. All the fields will be full of crops and there'll be lots of food. But after that, there'll be seven years of famine—no food at all. You should put someone in charge of all your crops right away, so they can begin to fill the storehouses with grain. If you do that, by the time the famine comes, there will be plenty of food in Egypt for everyone."

"Joseph," said Pharaoh, "I can see that God has made you wise. I'm going to put you in charge."

For the next seven years, Joseph made sure that all the grain was carefully stored away. And when the famine came, many people traveled from far and wide to buy food in Egypt.

One morning a group of eleven brothers arrived at the palace and bowed down to Joseph. "Please, sir," they said, "we are here to buy corn for our families in Canaan." Joseph couldn't believe his eyes! It was his brothers!

Joseph burst into tears. "I am Joseph, your brother," he cried. "Is my father still alive?" His brothers were shocked and scared. They couldn't speak. They just nodded and trembled in disbelief.

"Don't be afraid," said Joseph. "I forgive you. I love you. Many bad things have happened in my life, but God, who has been with me every single day, has brought good from them. I will give you food and a new home here in Egypt."

And so it was that God's family, the Israelites, left Canaan, the land that God had promised them, and came to live in Egypt. But one day, God would find a way to bring them back …

I Wonder

… if God can still bring good out of bad situations.

… if it was hard for Joseph to forgive his brothers.

… how Joseph knew that God had never left him.

I wonder about
MIRIAM

Exodus 2:1–10 and 14:13–15:2

God's people had lived in Egypt for many years, but it was time to leave and return to the land God had promised them. It wasn't going to be easy—Miriam knew that. She stood on the bank of the Red Sea and looked at her brother as the water foamed and frothed below them. Moses stood tall, his long beard blowing in the wind, his arm holding the staff he'd carried with him ever since he'd begun leading the Israelites out of Egypt.

But there was no escaping now. They were all trapped, every one of them. In front of them lay the huge, wide waters of the Red Sea. In hot pursuit was

the entire Egyptian army, urged on by Pharaoh. He wasn't going to let the
Israelites escape! They were his slaves.

Miriam was scared. She closed her eyes and remembered another time, long
ago, when she and Moses had been together at a different water's edge. In her
mind, Miriam could still see her baby brother floating in the little basket down
in the River Nile—it had been the only safe place to hide him from the wicked
Pharaoh. But God had been watching over Moses then. And God was watching
over Moses now. Surely God would save them and help them escape, back to the
Promised Land.

Miriam opened her eyes when she heard her brother's voice shouting over the crashing waves. "Do not be afraid!" Moses cried. "God is with us. We will not have to fight this army. God is stronger. God will make a way!" And with that, Moses held his staff high over the Red Sea. Miriam watched in amazement as a mighty wind blew the waves back and held them there, like two giant curtains rippling in the wind.

"Go!" Moses shouted as he jumped down onto the path that had miraculously opened through the water. And all the Israelites swiftly followed, desperate to escape.

When all the Israelites safely reached the other side, the wind died down and the waters flooded back into place. The Egyptian army couldn't reach them now. Miriam sank to her knees in prayer, and the Israelites hugged each other and danced for joy. They were free. Moses was free. Miriam was free. Miriam jumped to her feet, reached for her tambourine, and waved it high above her head, skipping and singing from her heart.

God who made a way, God who set us free,
God who leads and loves and lives, God has rescued me!

Miriam smiled at Moses. God, who had watched over her brother every day, and who had found a way to lead him through the waters now, would continue to lead them. God's people were on their way back to the Promised Land.

I Wonder

... if God has been watching over me since I was a baby.

... how Pharaoh felt when he saw how powerful God was.

... if Miriam ever doubted God would help them.

I wonder about
RAHAB

Joshua 6:1–23

It was forty years since Moses had led God's people out of Egypt. For those long forty years they'd been wandering around in the desert, trying to find their way back to the Promised Land. And now here they were. Joshua, their new leader, stood on the hillside and looked toward Jericho, the city that stood between him and Canaan—the land God had

promised to Abraham, Isaac, and Jacob all those years before. But the walls of Jericho were tall and wide. How could they possibly get inside?

In the city of Jericho, Rahab leaned out of her window. There was no sign yet of the Israelites who were marching toward her home. But one day soon they would be here.

Everyone in Jericho had heard how powerful and strong the God of the Israelites was. They had heard the unbelievable stories of how God helped all those people escape from Egypt. If that mighty God was marching with the Israelites, Jericho's army stood no chance. Rahab was afraid. But she was excited too. If it was true that God could take a raging sea and miraculously transform it into a path, then maybe God could transform her life. She was ready for a change. Rahab wanted to know this God—the One who could work miracles.

Rahab opened her eyes just in time to see two men running over the hillside toward Jericho. They must be Israelite spies! Rahab ran downstairs, opened the door, and quickly beckoned the men inside.

"Are you Israelites?" she whispered. "Because if you are, I want to help you. You can hide here while you spy on the city. But there's one condition. When you return with the Israelite army and march into Jericho, save me. I want to know your great God and be part of God's family."

The men nodded in agreement, then followed Rahab upstairs to hide on her roof.

Two days later, the spies brought their report back to Joshua. "The city is strong and well protected," they said. "The walls are very thick. I don't know how we're going to get inside, Joshua. What's your plan?"

Joshua's plan was simple—he was going to follow God's advice, as impossible as it seemed. Joshua would do what God had told him to do.

"We're going to march around the walls," Joshua said. "We're just going to march."

"What? No fighting?" the spies asked.

"No. No fighting," said Joshua. "We don't need to. God will be fighting for us."

Early the next morning, Joshua assembled the Israelites. He stood on the hillside overlooking Jericho. "Israelites!" Joshua shouted. "We are God's people. This is our Promised Land! We are going to march around the city walls for six days. On the seventh day, we will circle Jericho seven times, blow our trumpets as loud as we can, and then wait to see what our great God will do. Do not be afraid. God is with us."

That day Rahab watched from her window as the Israelites, led by Joshua, came marching down the hillside toward Jericho. But they weren't carrying weapons—they were carrying trumpets! For six days they stomped and stamped around the walls. And on the seventh day, the mighty walls of Jericho came tottering and tumbling to the ground.

All the people who lived in Jericho tried to run for their lives. But not Rahab. The Israelite spies saved her, just like they promised. Rahab turned her back on Jericho, turned away from her old life, and turned toward God instead. And one day, many, many years later, out of Rahab's own family, a boy named David was born. He would grow up to become one of the greatest kings of Israel. Rahab never knew that part of her story. But God did.

I Wonder

... how I might be part of God's story.

... what paths God might open in my life.

... if the Israelites believed that the walls would really fall down as they marched.

I wonder about
RUTH AND NAOMI
Ruth 1–4

Naomi couldn't sleep. She lay awake as the tears trickled down her face. Her life felt like a huge puzzle, and none of the pieces would fit together. She was an Israelite, living in Moab, a foreign country. Her husband had died. And now her two sons had died. There was only one thing to do. She would go back to Israel—it was where she belonged.

Early in the morning, Naomi and Ruth, her daughter-in-law, packed their bags and set out on the road to Bethlehem. But they hadn't gone very far when Naomi turned to the young woman beside her and said, "Ruth, you don't need to come with me. You should stay here with your own people. There's no future for you in Israel. I'm old. I'll never have any more sons for you to marry. And I'll never have grandchildren either. My life is over. But you are young. Stay here, in Moab, find a new husband, and take care of yourself."

But Ruth got hold of her mother-in-law's hands. "Naomi," she said, kindly. "I'm not going anywhere. I'm staying with you. Wherever you go, I will go. Your people will be my people. And your God will be my God."

And so the two women carried on walking, down the long road to Bethlehem. But they weren't traveling alone. God was going ahead of them. God was taking all the pieces of Naomi's life and putting them together to make a beautiful picture that looked like this …

In Bethlehem, Boaz (who came from Rahab's family) fell in love with Ruth. They got married!

Ruth and Boaz had a baby called Obed.

Naomi had a grandson!

Obed had a grandson, called David.

David became a king!

From King David's family, Jesus Christ, the savior of the world would be born. There's no more beautiful picture than that.

I Wonder

... if God is traveling ahead of me.

... how God might fit the pieces of my life together.

... how Naomi felt when she had a grandson.

I wonder about
DAVID

Psalm 8:3–4 and 23; 1 Samuel 16:13; 17:1–50

All was quiet on the hillside. David squinted into the darkness, scanning the fields below for his flock of sheep. They were safe now. The bears and lions that had tried to snatch them would not return tonight. David had fought them off well. But just in case, David would keep his trusty slingshot right by his side as he slept. He was not afraid. This was his special time with God.

Who are you, God? David whispered into the night. *How did you
make the heavens? How long did it take your fingers to set the stars in place? How big
are your hands, that they can carry the moon? And who am I? How can you possibly
know me, when I'm just a young boy?*

Early the next morning David woke up to find his father shaking him by the shoulder. "David, wake up," Jesse said. "An important priest named Samuel just arrived at our home. He's asking to see you."

"What can a priest want with me?" wondered David. When they arrived at Jesse's house, there stood Samuel, holding a jar of anointing oil. David's seven older brothers, all lined up with their arms folded, were waiting to see what would happen. "Kneel down, David," said Samuel. "God has chosen you for something very special. One day you will be king of Israel."

David couldn't believe what he was hearing. Had God really chosen him for such an important task? What did this mean? David knelt in front of Samuel, and Samuel poured oil on his head. As it ran down over his shoulders, David knew that God's Holy Spirit was pouring over him. He didn't know what all this meant, but he knew one thing for sure: whatever he faced in the future, God would be with him.

If ever David needed to know that God was with him, it was now. David was standing on the hillside above the Valley of Elah, with the Israelite army. On the other side of the valley stood Goliath, a huge, scary, ugly giant. He belonged to the Philistines, who were the Israelites' fiercest enemies. For forty days Goliath had been striding to the edge of the valley, roaring like a lion across to the other side. "Who will fight me? Send out your best man. I'll show you who's strongest!"

The sun rose high in the sky and cast Goliath's enormous, dark shadow onto the valley below. The giant stood with his huge hands on his hips and roared with laughter when he saw the young boy standing on the opposite side. "Ha, ha, ha!" Goliath boomed. "Is that the best you've got? Do you *really* think you can beat me?"

But David was not afraid. "It's true that you're big," he shouted back. "But my God is bigger. And you might be strong. But my God is stronger. And I might be small, but my God will make you fall!"

And with that, David stepped into the dark valley, took his loaded slingshot, and catapulted one smooth stone high into the air. Goliath didn't know what hit him. He staggered backward and forward and then crashed, headfirst, into the valley below.

No one could believe it. The Israelites shrieked with joy and ran to lift David into the air in celebration. They carried him back to their camp where they feasted all night long. David had won.

David never forgot how God had been with him in the Valley of Elah. And one day, many years later, after he became king of Israel, David picked up his harp and wrote a song of praise to God, his shepherd and protector …

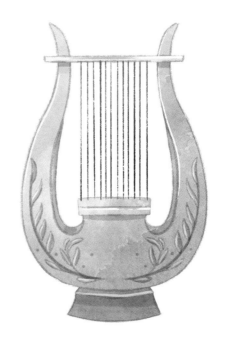

Even when the valley's deep
And even when it's wide,
I know my shepherd walks with me
And stays right by my side.
And when the darkest shadows
Make me feel afraid,
I hear my shepherd whisper,
"Do not be dismayed.
I'll lead you by still waters,
I'll help you find some rest."
And I will trust my shepherd,
The One who knows what's best.
We'll walk through life together
And every single day,
The goodness of my shepherd
Will guide me on my way.

I Wonder

… if there are any dark valleys or places where I wouldn't find God.

… how David really felt when he faced that giant.

… how God can see me, even though I'm small.

I wonder about
ELIJAH

1 Kings 6; 19:1–19

Everything was going well for God's people. They had settled happily in the Promised Land. They built homes, grew crops in the fields, and had families. King Solomon, David's son, built a beautiful temple in Jerusalem. Its golden roof gleamed in the sunshine for miles around and reminded the Israelites who they were: a special people who belonged to a special God. The temple was their favorite place to go to worship.

For forty years God's people lived in peace, and their enemies left them
alone. But soon after Solomon died, things started to go wrong. They started
fighting! They fought about who should be king, argued over who should own
the land, and quarreled about whether they should listen to God or not. They
fought so much that God's people couldn't stand the sight of each other. The
land of Israel was divided in two. Some of the Israelites went to the north, and
others went to the south.

God's heart was broken. This was not the dream God had for this special family! God wanted them to be together, not separated. They were supposed to love each other. So God decided to send some special messengers to Israel, messengers who would guide the people back to God's heart.

Elijah was sleeping when God came and spoke to him. "Elijah, get up. You will be the first of my special messengers. You'll be a prophet who will take my words to the people. Go to the Israelites and tell them to turn back to me."

But although Elijah tried and tried, no one would listen to his words. "You're a terrible troublemaker," they shouted. "We don't need God! We're not going to listen to your silly words. Get out of town!" And they chased after Elijah, waving their swords in the air. Elijah was terrified and ran for his life. He couldn't do this! How could he change peoples' hearts? How could he make a difference for God when no one would listen to him?

Elijah ran far, far away into the desert and took shelter under a broom tree. He sank to his knees in despair. "I've had enough, God," Elijah cried. "Just let me die, right here. I can't do what you asked. It's too hard." Then Elijah went to sleep.

As he slept, an angel came from heaven and touched him gently on the shoulder. "Elijah," the angel said. "You're not alone in this place. God is with you. Get up and eat so that you'll be strong enough for this hard journey."

Elijah thought he must be dreaming, but when he sat up, to his surprise, a small loaf of bread and a jar of water were sitting beside him. Elijah ate and drank. Early the next morning, as the sun rose over the trees, he set off running again, toward Mount Horeb. He knew there were caves in the mountain. It would be a good place to hide.

In the dark cave, bats were swinging, snakes were slithering, spiders were scuttling, and in the dark corner, Elijah was hiding. He'd been running for forty days and forty nights. He was tired and afraid, but Elijah knew that God would take care of him. After all, he was still God's messenger. God would find him here and help him. He just had to be patient. He would hear God's voice soon.

Suddenly, Elijah heard a great and powerful wind roaring outside the cave. The mighty wind tore the mountains apart and shattered the rocks. Elijah tiptoed closer to the entrance of the cave. Wow! Was that God's voice? But it wasn't. God was not in the wind.

Then Elijah heard a huge earthquake. Boom! The mountain shook and trembled under Elijah's feet. Wow! Was that God's voice? But it wasn't. God was not in the earthquake.

Then Elijah heard a fire—angry flames crackling and spitting, creeping and crawling over the rocks. Wow! Was that God's voice? But it wasn't. God was not in the fire.

Then Elijah heard a gentle whisper. The whisper came, dancing softly through the clouds, riding the breeze. The whisper came, flying high over the hills and through the trees. It crept into the cave. And if Elijah had not been listening carefully, he might never have heard it. Wow! Was that God's voice? Yes. It was. God was in the whisper. It was the same voice that had whispered the world into being.

Elijah pulled his cloak over his face and stepped out on the mountainside to meet God. God said, "Go back, Elijah. Go back down the mountain, back the way you came. I will give you a helper, another prophet who will help you bring my messages to the people."

Elijah hesitated. Could he go back, even though his life was in danger? Elijah nodded. If God would be with him, he could do it.

In the dark cave, bats were still swinging, snakes were still slithering, and spiders were still scuttling, but Elijah was gone. Elijah was running back down the mountainside, back the way he had come, his cloak flying out behind him in the wind. And God went with him.

I Wonder

... why God came in the whisper instead of the fire.

... what Elijah would have done if God hadn't come.

... if I could be God's messenger.

I wonder about
THE LITTLE SERVANT GIRL

2 Kings 1:11–13; 5:1–15

Elisha stood on the bank of the River Jordan. Then he peered up into the clouds, blinking his eyes and straining to see where Elijah had gone. He couldn't believe what had just happened. His friend, his teacher—the one who had taught him everything about God—had been whisked up into heaven in a chariot of fire! No one would believe him, but it was true. Elisha had seen it with his own eyes. It was up to him now. He was God's new messenger. He would try to be as good a prophet as Elijah had been.

In the far away land of Aram, the little servant girl opened the door of Naaman's house and swept the dust outside. She looked into the distance. Her home was so far away. She missed Israel. She missed her family. She hated crying herself to sleep at night. But the little servant girl didn't hate Naaman, her master. How could she hate anyone, when God had filled her heart with love? *I don't know why I'm here, God,* she whispered. *But I believe I'm going to go home one day. Until I do, help me to remember you. Help me to love.*

The little girl went into the kitchen to prepare Naaman's lunch. He would be home soon, and he was sure to be hungry. He worked hard every day. He was commander of the army of Aram. But even though he had a very important job, and even though he had a big house and lots of money, the little servant girl felt sorry for him. Naaman had leprosy—a horrible skin disease. He'd tried everything to get rid of it, but nothing worked. No medicine could cure it. But the little girl knew how her master could be healed. He just had to go and see Elisha, the prophet, who lived in Israel.

"Mistress," the little girl said to Naaman's wife, "I know a wonderful man called Elisha. He is God's messenger. With God's help, he can work miracles. I know that if my master went to see Elisha, God would heal him."

Naaman was so excited! Even though he didn't believe in the God of Israel, he'd heard good things about Elisha. It was worth a try.

Naaman saddled up his horses, climbed aboard his golden chariot, and galloped off to Israel with his servant. When he arrived at Elisha's little home, he turned to his servant, and said, "Go and knock on Elisha's door. Announce that the commander of the king of Aram's army is here and needs help to cure his leprosy." Then Naaman sat in his gleaming chariot and waited to meet Elisha. He looked toward the house and saw a glimpse of Elisha's cloak.

But a few seconds later, the servant returned—alone. "Well?" asked Naaman. "What happened? Where's Elisha?"

"Master," said the servant. "Elisha said you must go down to the River Jordan and dip in the water—not once, but seven times. Then God will cure your leprosy."

"What!" shouted Naaman. "Is he crazy? I'm not going anywhere near that smelly river! How could that dirty water possibly cure me? If I really thought a swim would help, I'd much rather go in one of the lovely rivers in my own land. Doesn't Elisha realize how important I am? I thought he would at least come out of his house, call upon his God, and wave his hand over my skin to cure me. I'm offended!"

"But, master," said the servant quietly, "we've come all this way. Why don't you just try it?"

Naaman grumbled and grouched. But eventually, he decided to do what Elisha had said. Slowly, he dipped his big toe in the River Jordan. It was freezing cold! And there were big catfish swimming nearby! But Naaman was a soldier. He was brave. If he could command the king's army, he could do this. Naaman plunged into the River Jordan seven times. And when he stepped out, it was a marvelous miracle! His leprosy was gone!

"Oh, my goodness me!" Naaman cried, as he examined his brand-new skin. He ran to Elisha's house and hugged him. "Elisha! You were absolutely right. Now I know that there's no god in all the world except the God of Israel."

Naaman returned home and told everyone he saw about how the God of Israel had healed him. The little servant girl was overjoyed when she saw how God had taken her master's leprosy away. And when she climbed into bed that night, for the very first time, she didn't cry herself to sleep.

Thank you, God, she whispered, *for helping me to love others. Thank you for healing Naaman. Now he knows that there's no God like you!*

The little servant girl closed her eyes and went to sleep. She had known that all along.

I Wonder

... why the little girl wanted Naaman to be healed.

... if she ever got to go home.

... if Naaman's belief in God continued to grow after he was healed.

I wonder about
JONAH

Jonah 1:1–3:3

It's no good, God. I'm not listening, Jonah thought. *Anyway, I must have heard you wrong. You can't possibly want me to go to Nineveh and tell those people that you love them. They're terrible! Plus, they're our worst enemies! You saw how they destroyed Jerusalem, wrecked Solomon's temple, and carried so many Israelites off to their own country. I can understand why you want them to change, but they surely don't deserve to be loved!*

"Jonah," God said calmly, "everyone deserves to be loved. If you take my message to the people there, they'll listen. They'll stop being mean. It will be a new chance for them. I'll forgive them."

But it was too late. Jonah had stopped listening. He'd already decided what to do. He was going to hide. He would run far, far away … so far that God wouldn't be able to find him.

Jonah sneaked out of his house and headed down to the beach. Just in time! There was a boat, all loaded up and ready to set sail for Tarshish. Perfect! Tarshish was in the opposite direction of Nineveh—just what Jonah wanted. So Jonah turned his back on God, turned away from Nineveh, and climbed aboard. He found a comfy hammock below deck, curled up, and went to sleep.

But it wasn't long before Jonah woke up. The captain of the ship was shaking his arm. His hammock was swinging wildly from side to side. "Jonah!" the captain cried. "How can you sleep when there's a terrible storm raging outside? We're all going to drown! You'd better pray hard to your God to save us."

Jonah went up on deck where the boat was pitching up and down in the waves. "This is my fault," Jonah shouted over the noise of the storm. "I shouldn't have tried to run away from God. Throw me overboard!"

The men picked Jonah up and tossed him into the deep waters of the Mediterranean Sea, but just as he was plummeting to the bottom, a huge fish came swimming toward him. It opened its massive mouth and swallowed him whole. Jonah somersaulted down its throat and landed upside down in the fish's belly. This was a terrible place to be! It was dark and smelly and wet and slimy. It was worse than being in Nineveh!

Jonah was inside that slimy, smelly belly for three whole days and three whole nights. While he sat in the dark, rolling about from side to side, he had plenty of time to think about what had happened. Perhaps he *should* go to Nineveh after all. It was wrong of him to ignore God. It was wrong of him to try to run away. He had hurt God. But God still loved him … Jonah was sure of that. And if God still loved Jonah, even though he'd done wrong, perhaps God did love the people of Nineveh too.

Jonah knew what he had to do. He wobbled to his knees, put his hands together, and prayed like he'd never prayed before. *Oh, dear God! Can you see me in here? Can you hear me in here? If you can, please save me and give me a second chance. I'm ready to do what you asked. I'm ready to go to Nineveh.*

No sooner had Jonah finished praying than the fish's big belly began to quiver and quake. The fish let out a gigantic hiccup. Jonah was catapulted from its belly and hurled out through its mouth. He landed headfirst on a beach.

As Jonah brushed the sand from his knees and set out for Nineveh, he thought about all the things God had taught him. He could run away from God, but he couldn't hide—even in a fish! God could hear his prayers, even from the depths of the deepest, darkest ocean. Most of all, Jonah knew that God had given him a second chance, just like the people of Nineveh would have a second chance. And everyone, *everyone* deserved God's love.

I Wonder

... if there's any place where God couldn't hear my prayers.

... if God really does love people who do wrong things.

... if I would have gone to Nineveh.

I wonder about
DANIEL

Daniel 6:1–28

In the land of Babylon there lived an Israelite called Daniel. Like so many of God's people before him, Daniel had been captured by a foreign army and taken far away from Israel. But even though he'd had to leave many things behind, there was one very important thing that Daniel brought with him—his faith in God. Daniel loved God. He listened to God, trusted God, and he prayed to God on his knees, three times, every single day.

In the royal palace where Daniel worked, he was the king's favorite. Daniel could do anything! If King Darius needed papers signed or special projects completed, he always chose Daniel for the task. Daniel was so trustworthy, dependable, and hardworking that King Darius planned to put him in charge of the whole kingdom.

"We'll soon see about that!" said some of the king's advisors, who were jealous of Daniel. "We're not going to have him in charge of us!" They came up with a wicked plan to get rid of Daniel.

"Oh, King Darius," the advisors said, as they bowed down in front of his throne. "May you live forever and ever! No other land in the world has a king as marvelous as you! We think that in honor of your greatness, you should make a special rule. Why not make a proclamation that for the next thirty days, everyone should pray only to you! If anyone is found praying to anyone else, he'll be thrown into the lions' den. It will be a wonderful way to celebrate your greatness!"

King Darius was very pleased. It sounded like a splendid idea to have all his subjects praying to him! He smiled, puffed out his chest, smoothed down his royal robes, and happily took the quivering quill that his advisors passed to him.

"Just put your royal signature right here, sire," they said, as they pushed the papers under his nose. No sooner had the king signed his name than the royal advisors scurried off with the papers and nailed one to every door in town. Then they waited.

Early the next morning the royal advisors sneaked up to Daniel's house and peeked through the window. Sure enough, there he was, on his knees, facing toward his beloved Jerusalem, praying to God. Daniel had read the proclamation that was nailed to his door. But it didn't matter. He was going to pray to his God anyway—out loud. The men outside spying could hear him!

"Dear God, thank you that you are the one, true, living God. Thank you for hearing my prayers for my people, the Israelites. Thank you for sending someone to help rebuild the walls of Jerusalem, so that we can worship you in that holy place once more."

The royal advisors rubbed their hands together in glee. Daniel had just broken the law! Now they could get rid of him!

They rushed back to the palace and bowed before the king. "Oh, King Darius, Your Greatness," they said. "We can't believe it! We just saw Daniel, on his knees, praying to his God! That means that according to the law which you, yourself signed, he must be thrown into the lions' den immediately!"

King Darius was so upset. He loved Daniel and knew at once that he'd been tricked. But the law was the law. It couldn't be changed. Nothing the king could do or say would save him.

So that very day, Daniel was thrown into a deep, dark den of hungry lions. A huge, heavy stone was rolled over the entrance to the cave. There was no way Daniel could escape.

All night long, King Darius tossed and turned in bed. At the crack of dawn, he jumped up, ran to the cave, and cried out, "Daniel! Has your God saved you?" And to his utter amazement, Daniel answered him.

"Yes, King Darius. I'm alive. My great God did save me. I was not alone in here. An angel stood by my side all through the night and kept me safe from the hungry lions."

King Darius was overjoyed! He hugged Daniel, called for his quivering quill, and wrote a note to all his kingdom.

By order of King Darius,
I hereby do declare,
That you must serve the living God
Who answered Daniel's prayer.
This is a God of miracles!
Whose hand set Daniel free.
A God who saves and rescues—
A God for you and me!

I Wonder

... why God sent an angel instead of just rolling the stone away from the den.

... why Daniel kept praying when he knew he would get in trouble.

... why people get jealous of each other.

I wonder about
NEHEMIAH

Nehemiah 2:11–6:15

Many years after Daniel had prayed to God for help, a wonderful thing happened. God's people were able to start returning to the land God had promised Abraham. The Israelites were overjoyed to be back in their homeland. They worked hard, day and night, to rebuild the golden temple King Solomon had built. God's people began to claim their Promised Land again.

But the city walls of Jerusalem that had once stood so proud and tall were in a terrible mess. Nehemiah crept along in the darkness with his men, shining his torch on what was left of the old city. All the stones from the walls were piled in big heaps. The mighty wooden gates lay crumbling and broken. It made Nehemiah cry. He'd been traveling for three long months, journeying back to his beloved home in Jerusalem, only to find that it was in ruins.

But Nehemiah was a man of God. He had been praying to God, and he knew that if God helped him, he could build those walls again. It wouldn't be easy, but once the city was rebuilt, all his family and friends could come back to live there, just like they used to.

There wasn't a moment to lose. Nehemiah gathered his team and his tools and carefully gave his instructions:

Pick up stones;
Stack them straight,
Climb up ladders,
Mend each gate.
Knock and nail,
Morn till night.
Build that wall …
Get it right!

But as they worked, their enemies were watching. They pointed their fingers and shouted at Nehemiah, "How silly! What makes you think you can rebuild those walls? You'll never do it. Your hands are too small and weak. Even if a fox climbed on that wall it would fall down!"

Nehemiah turned his back on his enemies and turned to God instead.
He put his hands together and prayed:

Oh, Lord God Almighty—let our hands be strong,
For we know with your help, this will not take long.

And guess what? After just fifty-two days, the wall was finished. The city wall was built again! Nehemiah's heart filled with joy as all his family and friends came back to live in Jerusalem. He looked up at the fox sitting safely on top of the wonderful wall. He looked down at his hands. He had small hands. But God had made them strong.

I Wonder

... what God might use my hands for.

... how God felt when Nehemiah's family came back to Jerusalem.

... if Nehemiah could have rebuilt the wall without God's help.

NOT THE END OF THE STORY

Now you might be thinking that this is a very happy ending. God's people were back in the Promised Land. The temple was rebuilt. Jerusalem's walls were strong again. But that wasn't the end of the story. The Israelites still forgot about God. They still fought with each other. They still had enemies. Most of all, they still didn't know how to love. God's people were lost, wandering about in the world like sheep without a shepherd.

But all through those long years, ever since God whispered the world into being and ever since God's children had stepped from their Creator's hand, God had never stopped speaking words of love and hope and future over them. God already had a plan. God knew how to put things right. It was the best plan of all.

God would open the gates of heaven and step down into the world. God would become their shepherd. And each one of God's whisper words, spoken throughout the years by all those faithful messengers, those wonderful whisper words would all come true—every single one of them …

Through Abraham: *I will bless you.*

Through Moses: *I will rescue you.*

Through Jeremiah: *I will give you hope and a future.*

Through Isaiah: *I will save you.*

Through Haggai: *I will bring you peace.*

Through Zechariah: *I will set you free.*

Through Malachi: *I will come to you.*

But how *would* God come to the world? Would the clouds open to let God charge out, like a mighty warrior on a horse? Would God float down from the sky, sitting on a golden throne, wearing a gleaming crown? Would trumpets blare and lights flash to announce God's arrival? No. God would come in the quiet of the night … in the stillness of a stable … like a whisper …

A child will be born to us.
A son will be given to us …
A Prince Who Brings Peace.

–Isaiah 9:6 NIrV

The Best Plan of All

NEW TESTAMENT

I wonder about
THE BIRTH OF JESUS

Luke 1:26–57; 2:1–20

The angel Gabriel quietly opened the gates of heaven and flew, like a feather, down to earth. He had a special message to deliver to a young girl named Mary, who lived in Nazareth.

Mary was sitting by the fire, thinking about God, when the whole room was flooded with light and Gabriel softly whispered her name. "Mary. God is with you."

Mary fell in fright to the floor and gazed up at the silvery wings fluttering in the firelight. She had never seen or heard an angel before. "Don't be afraid," Gabriel said. "You have been chosen for something wonderful. You will be the mama of God's Son. You must name your little one *Jesus*. He will grow up to be King of the whole world."

Mary couldn't believe what she was hearing. Could it really be true? "I don't understand," she said. "I'm not even married yet. And I'm so young."

"Don't worry, Mary," the angel said softly. "God can do anything! Even your relative, Elizabeth, is going to have a baby. And everyone said *she* was too old! But nothing is impossible with God."

What? Elizabeth was going to have a baby too? Mary could hardly believe it. But if it *was* true, how wonderful that would be! Mary smiled at the angel. "I'm God's servant," she whispered. "And no matter what happens, I'll always be God's servant."

Early the next morning, Mary jumped out of bed and set out for the little village on the hill where Elizabeth and Zechariah lived. She would soon find out from Elizabeth if what the angel had said was true. Hurrying to the door, she knocked. She heard Elizabeth's footsteps. As soon as Elizabeth saw Mary, she put her hand on her own tummy and cried out in surprise, "Mary! The baby inside me just jumped for joy! You're going to have a baby too—I just know it. How blessed you are!"

Mary gasped in amazement. So, it *was* all true! God's Holy Spirit danced as Mary hugged Elizabeth and sang for joy:

> *Oh, how my heart rejoices!*
> *Oh, hear my spirit sing!*
> *For I will have a little boy*
> *And he will be a King.*
> *I'll sing praise to my Savior,*
> *The Holy, Mighty One,*
> *And one day all the earth will know*
> *This great thing God has done!*

Mary stayed with Elizabeth for three months, and every day they marveled at what the angel had told them and wondered what their special sons would be like. When Elizabeth's boy was born, he was named John. And a few months later, it was Mary's turn to welcome her special son into the world.

Mary and Joseph had to take the long journey to Bethlehem to be registered there, but it was late when they arrived, and every single inn was full. The only place left for them was a small stable, full of animals. But at least it was warm. Mary lay down in the soft hay as Joseph covered her with a blanket.

Outside the little stable, the whole town of Bethlehem was asleep under the stars. For all the people curled up warmly in their beds, it was just an ordinary night. For all the animals snoozing quietly in the stable, it was just an ordinary night. But Mary and Joseph were awake. For them, this night was anything but ordinary. It was the night they welcomed God's own Son into the world.

Star shines down, stable small,
Mary's boy—born for all.
Shepherds wake, angels sing,
Wise men ready—gifts to bring.
Joseph smiles, Jesus sleeps,
Cows into the manger peep.
Star shines down, stable small,
Mary's boy—born for all.

Mary cuddled her newborn baby as he slept. As she listened to his soft, baby breaths, she gazed up into the deep blue sky, spread like a velvet blanket outside her window. If stars could sing, they were singing now. *Welcome, special one,* they seemed to say.

Mary thought about everything that had happened. Would her little boy really grow up to be a king?

Mary didn't know the answer, but as she looked at her boy as he lay, fast asleep, she knew one thing, for sure … if it was true, then this tiny treasure lying in her arms wasn't just God's gift to her. Jesus was God's gift to the whole world.

And nothing about that was ordinary.

I Wonder

… what angel Gabriel looks like.

… if there are still angels in the world.

… what it would have been like to be in the stable that night.

I wonder about
JOHN THE BAPTIST

Luke 3:2–22

When Elizabeth's son grew up, he lived in the desert. It was the place where John felt close to God. Somehow, inside, he had always known that God was real and when he sat, quiet with his thoughts, his heart told him that God had a special plan for his life—something only he could do. And one morning, he knew what that special plan was. John would be a messenger who would prepare the way for Jesus.

John jumped up from his tasty lunch of locusts and honey, grabbed his camel hair coat, and set off running for the River Jordan. John had heard God's voice, and he was ready. John knew exactly what God wanted him to do. And he shouted at the top of his voice:

Get ready, get ready, make way, make way!
A special one's coming—it might be today!

"Who is it, John?" asked the people. "Who's coming?"

"Someone wonderful," said John, as he waded out into the middle of the river. "Someone who can take all the bad things we've ever done and put them right. Someone who can teach us how to love and forgive. Someone who can change the world. And it's my job to get you ready for him. Are you ready to share what you have? Are you ready to change? Are you ready to be baptized? Then jump in the water and show me you're ready to be made new and clean."

All the people waded into the River Jordan, and John baptized them in the cool water. "Are we clean now?" they asked.

"You're clean on the outside," said John. "But only that special person can make you clean on the inside. When *he* baptizes you, you will feel like brand-new people."

How exciting! The people were ready. John was ready. And one wonderful morning, that special person came. Jesus came to the Jordan, stepped into the river, and was baptized by John. And when Jesus came up out of the water, the heavens opened, and a beautiful white dove flew softly down and landed on him. God's voice rang out loud and clear and strong and said, "You are my son. I am pleased with you."

Jesus was ready now to help everyone feel like brand-new people—ready to change the world.

I Wonder

... why Jesus decided to be baptized.

... how John felt when he baptized Jesus and heard God's voice.

... why a dove flew down and landed on Jesus.

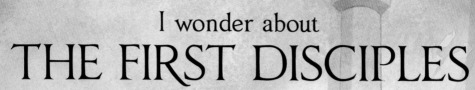

I wonder about
THE FIRST DISCIPLES

Luke 4:16–21; Mark 1:16–20 and 2:13–14

It was so quiet in the synagogue in Nazareth that you could have heard an ant sneeze. Everyone was silent. Their eyes fixed on this new teacher, a young man named Jesus. He picked up the scroll that had been written by the prophet Isaiah many, many years before, unrolled it, and read these words …

God's Spirit is upon me,
I bring good news today,
For those who walk in darkness
And cannot find their way.
God's Spirit is upon me,
To set the prisoners free.
I'll feed the poor and hungry,
And all the blind will see.

For a moment, everyone was silent. They couldn't believe the words they were hearing. It sounded like Jesus wanted to change the world. But how could he do that? "Wait a minute," someone cried. "Aren't you Mary and Joseph's son? How are *you* going to make Isaiah's words come true? Do you really think you can change the world, all by yourself?"

But Jesus wasn't worried. He already knew that he would need lots of help to teach people how to love and care for each other. And so, he went to a little town called Capernaum, on the banks of Lake Galilee. He knew he would find the right kind of people there.

Now you might think that Jesus, the Son of God, would need very special people to be on his team—perhaps important people with loads of money and big homes. But Jesus just needed ordinary people with big hearts with lots of room to learn about God's love. And the very first place that Jesus went was the beach.

There, on the shore, he saw two fishermen, working hard to mend their nets. "James and John," Jesus called. "Will you come with me and learn about God's love? Will you help me change the world?" The two brothers looked at each other, dropped their nets in the sand, and went with Jesus.

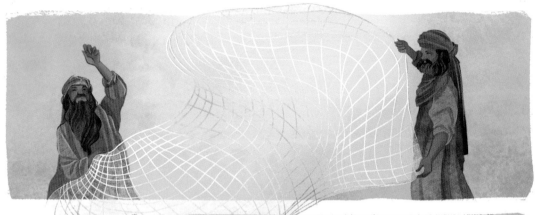

It was the same with Matthew. He left the little booth where he collected taxes, and followed Jesus.

Simon and Andrew, two more fishermen, did the same.

Jesus found twelve good men who were ready to listen to his words and teach others how to love. They were his first disciples. They were ordinary people, but they would do extraordinary things for God.

I Wonder

... if Jesus still needs disciples.

... if I could help to change the world.

... how I could help poor people.

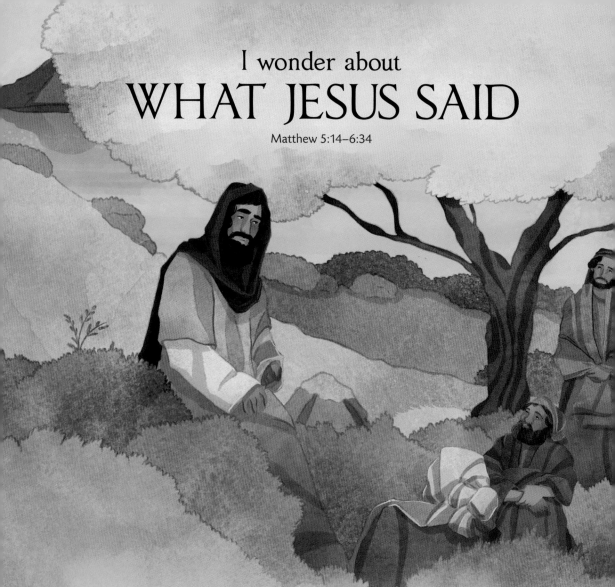

I wonder about
WHAT JESUS SAID

Matthew 5:14–6:34

On a hillside above the town of Capernaum, a crowd of people sat quietly on the grass. Sunlight sparkled on Lake Galilee below and little fishing boats bobbed up and down as the crowd listened to Jesus.

"The most important thing for you to know is that God is a God of love," Jesus said. "God loves you more than anyone or anything else in the whole world. And once you are filled with that love, you'll be like a bright light shining in the dark.

"Close your eyes. Imagine it's nighttime. Imagine that everyone here on the hillside—me, my disciples, every woman, every man, and every child—is holding a candle in the darkness. We'd be like a city that's shining on the hill. Our light would be so strong and bright that everyone for miles around would see it. You couldn't hide it! Let your light shine! Let your hearts shine with God's great love! And then love others—not just your family, not just your friends. God wants you to love everyone you meet—even your enemies! Can you imagine what the world would be like if we all did that?"

All the people on the hillside were listening. They'd never heard a message like this before. Even the birds stopped singing and the flowers turned their heads in the breeze to listen.

"Love your enemies. Be kind to them. Pray for them. And when you pray, don't stand up in the synagogue and shout your prayers, so that everyone around can hear. Whisper your prayers. God is listening. And pray like this ...

Our God, who is in heaven,

May your name be great.

May your kingdom come on earth,

Help us love, not hate.

May your will be always done.

Feed us, God, we pray.

And help us forgive others,

Like you forgive each day.

Don't lead us down a path that's wrong,

Help us know what's true

For yours, God, is the kingdom,

It all belongs to you.

No one spoke. No one moved. Everyone waited to hear what Jesus would say next. And Jesus pointed to the birds perched in the trees above. "Just look at the birds of the air. God loves them. God feeds them. But how much more important are you than the birds? Just look at the lilies of the field. How beautiful are they? If God clothes them like that, won't God take care of you? So, don't worry about your life. Don't worry about what to eat or what to wear. Put God first. And God will take care of everything you need."

A great calm and peace settled on the hillside above the little town, and everyone knew that Jesus' words were true.

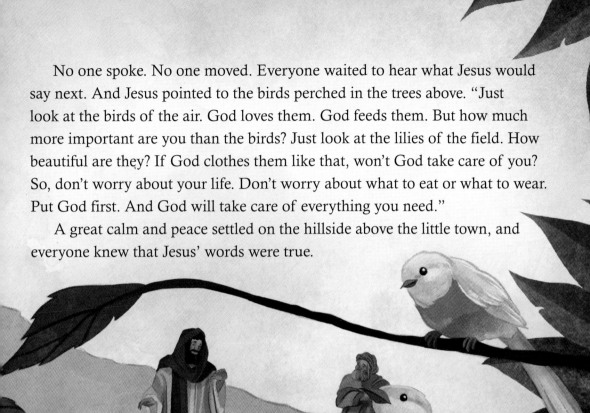

And that night, all around Capernaum, there were people praying for their enemies before they went to bed and being kind and practicing goodness. And they weren't worried about tomorrow as they fell asleep, because they knew that God, to whom they were much more important than the birds or the flowers, was holding them.

The world was changing.

130

I Wonder

... how I could let my light shine in the world.

... what it would be like to hear Jesus teaching.

... how I can put God first.

131

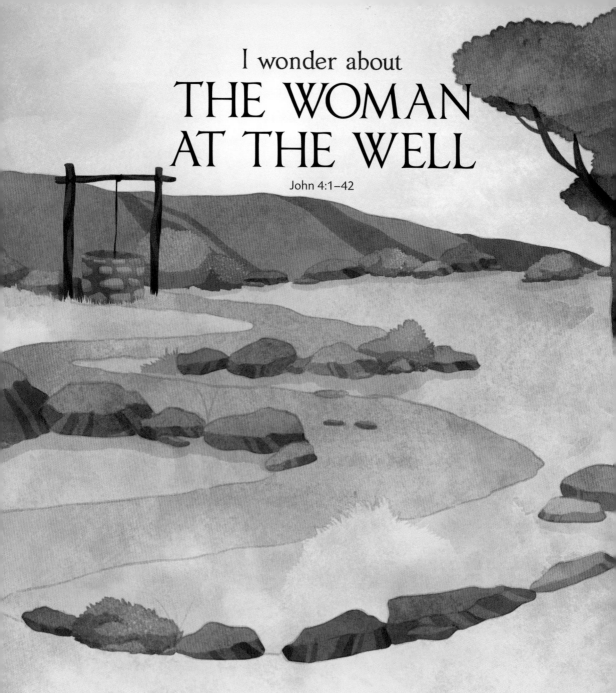

I wonder about
THE WOMAN AT THE WELL

John 4:1–42

The Samaritan woman woke up early and her heart filled with sadness. There was no point getting up yet. Today would be just the same as yesterday, and every day before that.

132

For as long as she could remember, she'd had the same routine: get up; lift the heavy water jar; go out in the burning noon-day sun; go to the well; fill the jar with water; carry it home. That jar felt as heavy as her heart. She felt as if her lonely life had no meaning, no purpose, and no peace. But she dragged herself out of bed and set out for the well.

But what the woman didn't know was that Jesus was sitting by the well, waiting for her. Her life was about to change …

The hot sun beat down on the woman as she made her way to Jacob's well. All the other women went there early in the morning, when it was cooler. But it was better for her if she went alone. After all, no one in town liked her. When she reached the well, she was surprised to see a man sitting there. She pulled her cloak tighter around her face. He was a Jew—she could tell that by the clothes he wore, and Jews hated Samaritans. She would fill her jar quickly and leave. But the man spoke to her. "Could you please get me a drink?" The woman was shocked. Why was he talking to her?

"Sir," she said. "I'm a Samaritan. You are a Jew. You don't know me."

"But I *do* know you," Jesus said softly. "I know you're unhappy. I know you've had five husbands. I know you've been searching for love. But you don't have to search anymore."

What did he mean? Who was this man who knew all about her, who had hope in his words and healing in his voice?

"Look at this well," Jesus said, kindly. "God's great love for you is deeper than the deepest well, wider than any ocean, and longer than any river. The love God has for you is like a stream of living water that can never run dry. When you drink that kind of water, you'll never be thirsty again."

"Sir," the woman said, "where can I find this living water? I know that when God's messenger, Jesus Christ, comes he will explain all this to me."

"I am he," whispered Jesus. The woman's heart skipped a beat. It was as if the cactus at her feet burst into bloom. This was Jesus Christ! The woman sprang to her feet, left her water jar, and ran into town, shouting to everyone who would listen. "I have met the Messiah, the Christ. Come and meet him too!"

Everyone in the whole town poured out into the streets to listen to the woman's story and meet Jesus for themselves. And every day after that, instead of waking up with sadness in her heart, the woman woke up filled with joy. She knew that God's great love for her would never run dry. She had a wonderful story to tell, and her life had meaning, purpose, and peace.

I Wonder

... what the most important part of this story is.

... why everyone in the town wanted to hear the woman's story.

... how it is that God's love can never run out.

I wonder about
THE MAN WHO COULDN'T WALK

Mark 2:1–12

The little house where Jesus was staying with his disciples was so full that not even a mouse could squeeze inside. The whole town of Capernaum was there, spilling outside into the street and crowding around Jesus as he taught. Suddenly, Jesus stopped talking. Above his head came strange sounds of scratching and scraping, bumping and banging. Someone was on the roof! All the people looked up in amazement as pieces of mud and straw began to fall on their heads.

The crowd shaded their eyes and watched as a hole began to appear above them. The hole got bigger and bigger, until blue sky appeared, and then four little faces peered over the edge of the hole. "Jesus," the four men called down. "We couldn't get through the door, so we decided to come through the roof. We've brought our friend. He can't run, or hop, or even walk, so we picked him up on his mat and brought him to you. We know you can make his legs better. Here he comes!"

And with that, the four friends started to lower the man on his mat down.
With a bump, the mat landed at Jesus' feet. Jesus looked up at the four friends
who were peering through the hole. He looked at the man, who was looking
hopeful. He looked at all the people in the house, who were covered with bits of
straw and mud. And Jesus laughed. "Pick up your mat," he said. "It's time to
go home."

And for the very first time in his life, the man stood up. His legs worked! The four friends on the roof nearly fell through the hole as they jumped for joy. The man picked up his mat and began running, as the crowd clapped and cheered. Everyone looked at Jesus in amazement. Here was a man who could bring healing, hope, and happiness to everyone's hearts.

I Wonder

... how I could be a good friend today.

... if that house in Capernaum is still there.

... what the man did when he went home.

I wonder about

THE SON WHO CAME HOME

Luke 15:11–24

One day, Jesus told a story about a son who wanted to leave home and travel around the big, wide world. This son gathered up all his money, packed his bags, and set off. He felt *so* excited to be leaving home, but his dad felt very sad. His dad stood on the doorstep, put his hand above his eyes so that he could see all the way down the long, winding road, and waved goodbye to his son.

The son traveled for many days until he came to a new country. He spent lots of money on new clothes, food, and games. This was fun. But while he was having fun, do you know what his dad was doing? His dad stood on the doorstep, with his hand above his eyes, looking all the way down the long, winding road, watching and waiting to see if his son was coming home.

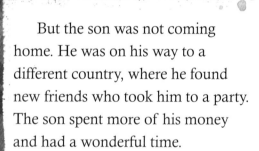

But the son was not coming home. He was on his way to a different country, where he found new friends who took him to a party. The son spent more of his money and had a wonderful time.

While the son was at that party, do you know where his dad was? His dad stood on the doorstep, with his hand above his eyes, looking all the way down the long winding road, watching and waiting to see if his son was coming home. But the son was not coming home.

Many months passed until one day, the son realized that all his money was gone. All his friends were gone. All his food was gone. He had to work in a smelly pigpen. And he was *so* hungry, but all he had to eat was the smelly pigs' food.

While the son was deciding what to do, do you know what his dad was doing? His dad still stood on the doorstep with his hand above his eyes, looking all the way down the long, winding road, watching and waiting to see if his son was coming home.

This time, he *was* coming home! As the son walked slowly up the road, he was worried. What if he'd traveled so far away that his dad had forgotten about him? But that dad was running down the long, winding road to welcome home the son he loved! What a fantastic father! As his dad hugged and hugged him, the son realized that no matter how far away he traveled, he could never, ever travel away from his father's love. The son was home.

I Wonder

... if the dad would ever have given up waiting for his son.

... how the son felt when his dad hugged him.

... if God is like that father.

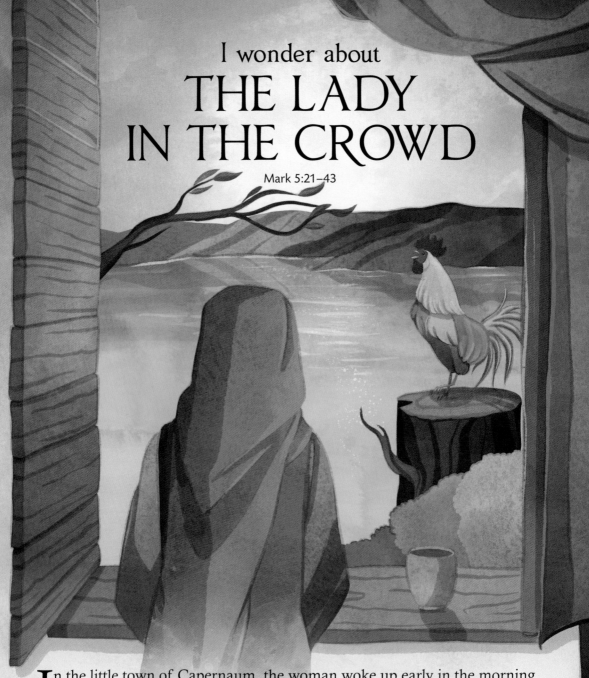

I wonder about
THE LADY
IN THE CROWD

Mark 5:21–43

Ⅰn the little town of Capernaum, the woman woke up early in the morning. Would today be the day she would be cured? For twelve long years she'd been ill. No doctor could cure her. No medicine could help her or take her pain away. Her hope was gone. But maybe, just maybe, today would be different.

The woman had heard about Jesus. He wasn't really a doctor. He didn't charge any money or give medicine. He didn't have an office or take appointments. You just went to him on the street, or wherever he was. And all he did to make you better was speak, or touch you, or pray for you. And you were healed. Jesus sounded amazing. Was it too good to be true? The woman didn't know, but she would find out today.

On the beach beside the Sea of Galilee, a huge crowd gathered around Jesus to hear him teach. The woman hobbled up and joined the crowd. But just as she was trying to decide how to get to Jesus, an important man from the synagogue came rushing through the crowd and fell at Jesus' feet. "Jesus!" he cried. "My little daughter is about to die. Please, come and heal her. Now!" Jesus immediately began to follow Jairus through the streets, and all the crowd hurried behind.

The woman sobbed in despair. How could she get to Jesus now? She couldn't delay him. Jairus was a leader in the church. She didn't feel like she was as important as him. But this was her only chance! If only she could just touch Jesus' clothes, then perhaps she would be healed.

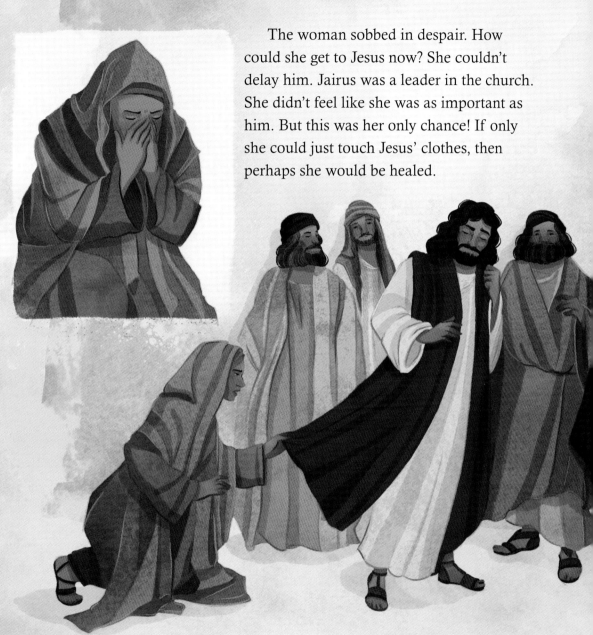

The woman plucked up the courage, bent down, and touched the hem of Jesus' robe as he passed. Immediately, all her pain was gone, and she knew she was completely healed. But Jesus stopped and turned around. "Who touched me?" he asked. The crowd fell silent.

"Jesus," Peter said. "Look at the crowd. Everyone's pushing. Lots of people touched you."

"No," Jesus said, softly. "You don't understand. Someone important touched me. Someone who needs me."

The woman was scared. Trembling, she fell at Jesus' feet and said, "It was me, sir. I touched you."

Jesus bent down and smiled. As the woman looked deep into his eyes, she saw that there was no anger there—only love, hope, and healing. "My daughter," Jesus said, "your faith has made you well. Go in peace."

As Jesus made his way to Jairus's house, the woman ran home with a skip in her step and a song in her soul. She would never forget what had happened today or what Jesus had said. He had called her *daughter*. She belonged to his family! She was every bit as important to Jesus as Jairus was. And that day, Jesus hadn't just healed her body. Jesus had healed her heart.

I Wonder

... why the woman didn't think she was as important as Jairus.

... if I'm important to Jesus.

... if everyone in the whole world is important to Jesus.

I wonder about
THE FARMER

Matthew 13:1–23

"Once upon a time," Jesus said, "there was a farmer who owned a big, beautiful farm. Day after day he grew wonderful flowers, fruits, and vegetables.

"One morning the farmer went out to sow some seeds. He reached into his bag, grabbed four little seeds, and flung them high in the air. As they tumbled down, the little seeds were excited to see where they would land.

"The first little seed fell on the path. When he saw a greedy bird flying down to gobble him up, that seed knew he was in trouble. 'Oh, no! I can't grow!'

"The second little seed fell in a rocky place. When he saw that the hot sun was about to dry him up, he was in trouble too. 'Oh, no! I can't grow!'

"The third little seed fell among some prickly thorns. When he saw a nasty weed wrapping itself around him, that little seed knew he was in trouble. 'Oh, no! I can't grow!'

"But the fourth little seed fell on good, deep soil. When he saw that this was a great place to grow, that little seed knew he was *not* in trouble. 'Oh, yes! I'm in the best spot to grow!' He grew and grew into a big, beautiful flower. And when the farmer saw it, he was *so* happy."

Jesus finished his story and looked out at the crowd.

"Now," said Jesus. "Did you know that I'm like the farmer? My words are like his seeds, and your heart is like his field. But when I sow my words in your heart, I don't want to grow lentils. I want to grow love. I don't want to grow potatoes. I want to grow peace. I don't want to grow carrots. I want to grow kindness.

Now can love, peace, and kindness grow in a heart that's hard and rocky and choked with worries? No. Love, peace, and kindness grow in a heart that's like that good, deep soil—in a heart that's ready to receive my words and listen to them.

And guess what?" Jesus said, as he looked out at everyone who was listening. "That's just what *you're* doing right now. Love is growing in your hearts like big, beautiful flowers, and just like the farmer was happy, that makes me so happy too."

I Wonder

... if I can make Jesus happy.

... if my heart is like a beautiful garden.

... how farmers feel when they see their seeds growing.

I wonder about
THE HUNGRY CROWD

John 6:1–13

The early morning sun rose high over the hillside where Jesus sat with his disciples and a huge crowd of people. Wherever Jesus went, a crowd followed. Everyone wanted to listen to him. The stories he told filled their hearts with peace and brought them closer to God. The little children ran up the hillside, because they knew that Jesus loved them, and they'd be able to sit on his lap as he talked about God. Those who were sick, those who couldn't walk properly, those who needed help, they all clambered up the hillside, because they knew that Jesus would heal them.

All day long, the people sat and listened to Jesus. His words were so wonderful that time passed quickly. No one thought about eating dinner, because they were too interested in what Jesus had to say. But when the sun started to go down, they were hungry.

Jesus turned to Philip and said, "Where shall we buy bread for these people to eat?"

Philip laughed. "Jesus," he said, "If I worked for eight months, I still wouldn't have enough money to buy bread for this crowd! There's over five thousand."

But Andrew had noticed a little boy, who shyly stepped forward, holding out his lunch. It was only five small loaves of bread and two tiny fish.

"Are you willing to share?" Jesus asked the boy. The little boy nodded and watched in amazement as Jesus took the bread, broke it, thanked God, and began to pass his lunch around. The bread never ran out. The fish never ran out. More bread appeared. More fish appeared. Until every single person on the hillside had as much as they wanted. The boy looked at Jesus. He couldn't believe it. Jesus had taken his little lunch and turned it into a mighty, miraculous meal.

And every single person on the hillside went home not just with their tummies full, but their hearts full as well.

I Wonder

... if I would have shared my lunch that day.

... if the little boy remembered what had happened when he grew up.

... what would have happened if the boy had kept his lunch for himself.

I wonder about
JESUS WALKING ON WATER

Matthew 14:22–32

Peter's heart was beating fast. He gripped the side of the little boat and watched as big waves began to splash over the edge. The storm was getting worse. Peter and the disciples needed help. But who knew where they were? They were all alone in the darkness on the lake. No one could see them. If they shouted for help no one would hear them. The storm was too loud. And where was Jesus? He was far, far away, praying on the mountainside.

Suddenly, Peter got the fright of his life. Right in the middle of those crashing waves, someone was walking on the water! The disciples were so afraid they nearly jumped overboard. "It's a ghost, it's a ghost!" they cried. But ghosts cannot talk.

"Friends, don't be scared. It's me. It's Jesus."

Oh, boy! It was Jesus! Jesus was walking on the water! Peter couldn't believe it. "Can I do that too, Jesus?" he shouted.

Jesus nodded and smiled. The other disciples watched in amazement as
Peter climbed overboard and started to walk on the waves. One step, two steps ...
"Here I come!" Peter shouted.

But then, Peter stopped thinking about Jesus. And instead he started to think about the scary place he was in. He started thinking about the wind and the waves. His heart started beating fast. Peter wobbled. And Peter started to sink! But as soon as he shouted for help, Jesus held out his big, strong hand and pulled him up, out of the water. When they climbed back in the boat, the storm vanished.

Peter lay in the little boat. He looked at Jesus and thought about what had happened that night. Jesus had known where they were all along. Jesus had eyes that could see in the darkest dark and ears that could hear above the loudest storm. And Jesus had the biggest, strongest hand that Peter had ever held.

The waves weren't crashing anymore. Peter's heart wasn't beating fast anymore. And that was called peace. Jesus had brought him peace.

I Wonder

... if there's any place too dark for Jesus to see.

... how Peter felt when he walked on the water.

... what might help me think about Jesus when I'm in a scary place.

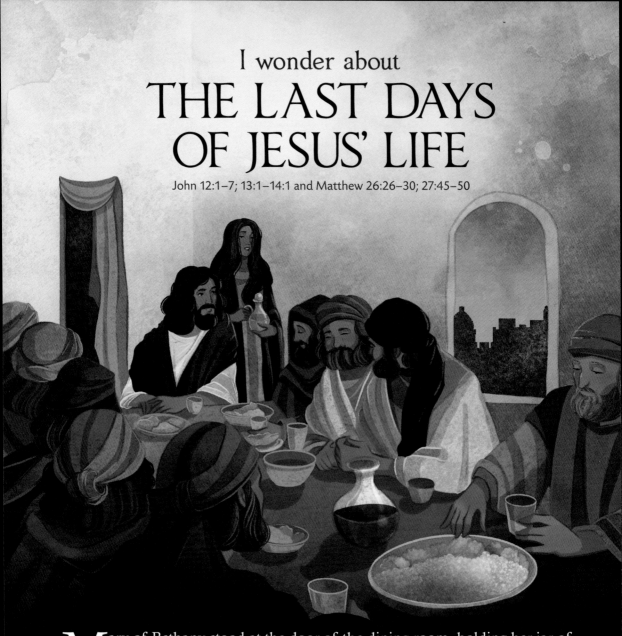

I wonder about
THE LAST DAYS OF JESUS' LIFE

John 12:1–7; 13:1–14:1 and Matthew 26:26–30; 27:45–50

Mary of Bethany stood at the door of the dining room, holding her jar of perfume, and wondered if she was brave enough to go inside. She could see Jesus, Lazarus, and all the disciples gathered around the table, eating and talking. She really wanted to do something special for Jesus—he had been so good and kind to her. And if all the rumors she'd heard were true, his enemies were trying to find a way to get rid of him.

Mary plucked up courage, pushed the door open, and tiptoed up to Jesus. Taking her jar of oil, she quietly poured it over his feet and then dried them with her hair. The sweet smell of perfume floated up from the floor and crept into every corner of the house. The men at the table stopped talking and looked at Mary in surprise.

"What on earth are you doing?' cried Judas, in disgust. "That perfume is SO expensive! What a waste!"

But Jesus smiled at Mary and spoke up for her, just like he always did. "Leave her alone. What Mary has done for me today will always be remembered. She has washed my feet, ready for the day I die. It wasn't a waste—it was wonderful."

A few days later, Jesus and his disciples gathered in an upstairs room in Jerusalem. Jesus knew he didn't have long to live, but he still had some important things to teach his disciples as they shared this last meal together. Reaching for the bread, Jesus broke it and said softly, "Whenever you eat bread, remember me."

Then he took the wine, poured it out and said quietly, "Whenever you drink wine, remember me." The disciples were worried. Was Jesus going to leave them?

"Children," Jesus said, softly. "Don't let your hearts be troubled. Don't be afraid. You will see me again one day, and you'll have so much joy that no one will be able to take it away. But until that day, the most important thing you can do is to love one another—just like I love you."

And then Jesus got up from the table, wrapped a towel around his waist, and began to wash the disciples' feet, just like a servant would do. The disciples couldn't believe it. Here was the King of the World, the Prince of Peace, the Mighty One, kneeling on the hard floor, taking their dirty feet in his hands and washing them, just like Mary of Bethany had done for him a few days before.

"It's all about love," Jesus said. "Love others—as strong as you can and as long as you can. Then everyone in the whole world will know that you are my disciples."

When evening came, Jesus and his disciples left the upper room and walked to the Garden of Gethsemane. And there, in the darkness, the soldiers came with torches and weapons and led Jesus away.

The next day, at 3 o'clock in the afternoon, the sun stopped shining. The sky turned dark. Heavy clouds of sadness hung in the air. Thunder roared. Trees trembled. The whole earth began to shake. And high on a hillside, on the cross, Jesus said goodbye.

Goodbye, world,
Goodbye trees,
Goodbye sunsets,
Goodbye seas.
Goodbye friends,
Goodbye Mom
Goodbye world.
And everyone.

"It's all finished," whispered Jesus. And he closed his eyes and died.
Except—Jesus wasn't finished.
And neither was God …

I Wonder

… why the sun stopped shining.

… how God felt when Jesus died.

how Jesus' friend Mary felt when Jesus died.

I wonder about
THE DAY JESUS CAME BACK ALIVE

John 20:1–18

It was still dark when Mary Magdalene woke. She opened her eyes and remembered, sadly, what had happened just three days before. Her best friend, Jesus, had died. Mary had seen him die on the cross; she'd followed Joseph of Arimathea and Nicodemus as they'd carried his body to a quiet cave on the hillside; she'd stayed there and watched them roll the big stone over the entrance. Mary had been with Jesus to the very end, and now she would go back to the cave and anoint his body with perfume.

But what Mary didn't know was that high on the hillside, the sun had already started to shine again. The sky was blue and bright and beautiful. No clouds could be seen. Only sunlight and hope and joy whispered in the air. And on that promise-filled morning, before Mary arrived at the tomb, what would have been impossible for anyone except God, happened. Jesus came alive again! Jesus stepped out from the dark cave and, with a big smile on his face, said hello to the world.

Good morning, world,
Good morning, trees,
Good morning, sun,
Good morning, seas!
Good morning, friends,
Good morning, Mom,
Good morning, God,
New life's begun.

When Mary arrived at the cave, she knew something had happened. The big stone was gone and when she peeked inside, she saw that Jesus' body was gone too. Mary sank to her knees in despair and began to cry. But above the sound of her sobs, someone was calling her name. Mary turned around and saw a man who she thought must be the gardener. But only one person said her name like that. "Mary. Mary. It's me. It's Jesus."

Suddenly, Mary's sadness was gone. Into her world, the Light came, flooding and leaping and dancing into the darkness, chasing away all the shadows and shining into every corner of her heart. Jesus was alive!

"Go, Mary," Jesus said softly. "Go and tell the disciples the Good News. Tell them that I am alive!"

Mary ran, without stopping, to the upper room in Jerusalem. She burst through the door and told the disciples what she had seen and heard.

Jesus was alive! And now, Mary and all the disciples had work to do. They had to go out and tell the whole world the wonderful story of Jesus. And they did.

I Wonder

... how I would have felt if I'd peeked into that empty cave.

... how Mary felt when she realized Jesus really was alive.

... what this story has to do with my life.

I wonder . . .
WHAT HAPPENED NEXT

Acts 9:1–22; 16:13–15

Are you wondering what happened next in the wonderful story of Jesus? From the moment Jesus stepped out of that quiet cave, the world was never the same. Beginning with Mary Magdalene, the Good News about Jesus and his love spread from door to door, from street to street, from town to town, and from country to country. And whenever and wherever ordinary people heard about Jesus, they did extraordinary things for God.

A man named Saul who heard God's voice in a blinding light on the road to Damascus changed his name to Paul and traveled all over the world to tell other people about Jesus. He was thrown in prison, but that didn't stop him—he picked up his pen and wrote letters to all the churches, encouraging them to follow Jesus. He was shipwrecked, but that didn't stop him—he swam to shore, jumped on another ship, and continued his mission. He was beaten, but that didn't stop him—he picked himself up, put bandages on, and carried on preaching. For as long as he lived, Paul never stopped preaching and teaching about Jesus.

A woman named Lydia was one of the first to hear Paul talk about Jesus as she sat by the river one day.

As soon as Paul started speaking, Lydia heard God's quiet voice calling out to her heart; she felt God's Holy Spirit all around—rustling in the leaves and dancing in the breeze. She ran home, gathered together everyone who lived in her house, and rushed back down to the river, where they were all baptized. Every day after that, Lydia opened her home to others who wanted to know about Jesus too. Her home became one of the first Christian meeting places in the world.

And two thousand years later, wherever we are, whatever we're doing, no matter who we are or how we're feeling …

whether young or old,

whether sleeping or awake,

whether active or still,

whether happy or sad,

whether alone
or together …

God is still reaching out to us—calling out in that quiet voice to all who will listen.

And for all who will hear, and for all who will respond, the wonderful story of Jesus is still being told.

I Wonder

… why Paul didn't give up telling others about Jesus
when all those bad things happened to him.

… if Lydia ever imagined that her story would one day be told to others.

… if God is reaching out to me.

EPILOGUE

I wonder about
YOU

Even though so many years have passed since Paul met Jesus in that blinding light on the road to Damascus and Lydia came to know Jesus Christ down by the river, every day, from then until now, Jesus Christ has been shining his light in the world and meeting people where they are. Wherever you are as you read this book, whether you're sitting in a quiet room, traveling along the road, or reading by a river, know that God's Holy Spirit is all around; know that God's quiet voice is calling out—across the centuries, across the seas—calling out to *you*.

Like every one of those disciples—like Mary Magdalene and Peter, Lydia and Paul—*you* are part of God's great story too.

Listen for God's quiet voice.
Watch for God's Holy Spirit at work in your life.
Wonder about the One who is calling you.

Listen, Watch, and Wonder—and God will do great things through *you*.

I Wonder...

... if God's Holy Spirit is with me right now.

... where I might find it easiest to listen to God.

... what great things God might do through me.